W9-ABU-035

Fact Finders®

EXTREME LIFE

POOP-EATERS
DUNG BEETLES IN THE FOOD CHAIN

BY DEIRDRE A. PRISCHMANN

Consultant:
Gary Dunn, Director of Education
Young Entomologists' Society
Minibeast Zooseum
Lansing, Michigan

Capstone
press®

Mankato, Minnesota

Fact Finders are published by Capstone Press,
1710 Roe Crest Drive, North Mankato, Minnesota 56003.
www.capstonepub.com

Library of Congress Cataloging-in-Publication Data
Prischmann, Deirdre A.
    Poop-eaters : dung beetles in the food chain/by Deirdre A. Prischmann.
    p. cm. — (Fact Finders. Extreme life)
    Summary: "Describes dung beetles, including development, place in the food chain, and how
they help the environment" — Provided by publisher.
    Includes bibliographical references and index.
    ISBN-13: 978-1-4296-1265-4 (hardcover)
    ISBN-10: 1-4296-1265-7 (hardcover)
    1. Dung beetles — Juvenile literature. I. Title. II. Series.
QL596.S3P82 2008
595.76'49 — dc22   2007020440

Editorial Credits

Jennifer Besel, editor; Alison Thiele, designer; Linda Clavel, photo researcher

Photo Credits

Ardea/Brian Bevan, 19
Bruce Coleman Inc./M.P. Kahl, 4–5
Capstone Press/Alison Thiele, 24 (pencil and paper)
Corbis/Chris Hellier, 15; Gallo Images/Paul Funston, 26–27; Martin Harvey, 14; Michael & Patricia
    Fogden, 8–9
Jupiterimages/David Curl, 18; Rob Nunnington, 25
Minden Pictures/FLPA/Nigel Cattlin, 12; PIOTR NASKRECKI, 7 (top right)
Photo Researchers, Inc/Dr. Morley Read, 20
Ronald G. Wolff, 13
Shutterstock/Chris Fourie, 21; EcoPrint, 7 (bottom left); Feng Yu, 11; Helder Joaquim Soares de
    Almeida, 7 (background); Jan Quist, 10; Joy Stein, cover, 17; Kmitu, 22–23; Larsek, 7 (bottom
    right); Nick Stubbs, 3 (both), 30, 31, 32
Trond Larsen, 28 (both) (Image on left features researcher Angelico Asenjo.)

TABLE OF CONTENTS

CHAPTER 1

WONDERFUL WASTE

Have you ever stepped in a pile of dog poop? Yeah, it's gross. Why do animals make such gross stuff? Animals get energy from the food they eat. They get rid of what they can't use in the form of poop.

Animals poop all over the place. But there aren't piles of poo everywhere. What happens to it? Well, something eats it. That's right. There's an army of poop-eating creatures out there. Those creatures are the dung beetles.

Dung beetles quickly find fresh piles of elephant poo. In less than a day, this pile will be all gone.

5

Feces and the Food Chain

Believe it or not, poop, and the creatures that eat it, are an important part of the food chain. What's the food chain? It's how energy flows between living things. Imagine the sun shining on a grassy field. Producers, like grass, make up the bottom of the food chain. Plants use sunlight to make their own energy. Then a **consumer**, like a hungry zebra, eats the plant. The consumer gets energy from the grass.

The waste the consumer leaves behind is energy for other animals. **Scavengers**, like dung beetles, scoop up and eat the moist **manure**. They get energy from poop! Dung beetles break down waste and return nutrients to the soil. Nutrients help plants grow, and the food chain starts again.

consumer: an animal, like a zebra, that eats plants or animals to get energy to survive

manure: another word for animal poop

scavenger: an animal, like a dung beetle, that eats dead animals or animal waste

SUNLIGHT

SCAVENGER

PRODUCER

CONSUMER

7

CHAPTER 2

THE SCOOP ON DUNG BEETLES

Animals live all over the world, and their cleanup crew is close behind. Where there's poop, there's a dung beetle! Most dung beetles live in tropical and subtropical areas where animal waste stays wet and fresh. But these scavengers are also found in drier places. There are about 7,000 **species** of dung beetles found around the world. They live everywhere except on Antarctica.

Some dung beetles live in habitats like forests, grasslands, or pastures. Many different animals live and deposit droppings in these places. Other dung beetles are found in habitats with only a few types of poop, like caves or animal burrows.

species: a specific type of insect, animal, or plant

Monkey poop is a favorite for dung beetles that live in the rain forest.

GROSS!

Some dung beetles live near sloth, monkey, or wallaby butts. The beetles eat poop sticking to the animals' fur.

Creature Features

Like all insects, dung beetles have six legs. They have hardened front wings called elytra. The elytra cover the delicate wings used for flying. Most dung beetles are black. But some are red, green, or copper colored. Adults range in size from smaller than a pencil eraser to bigger than a walnut.

TOP 5 AMAZING DUNG BEETLE TRAITS

1 Dung beetles don't drink water or eat food other than dung. They get all the nutrients they need from poop.

2 One dung beetle can bury more than 250 times its own weight in one night.

3 Dung beetles clean up after themselves by eating their own poop.

4 Scientists think dung beetles use moonlight to move in a straight line.

5 Dung beetles sometimes carry other animals from pile to pile. When a pile of poo becomes hard to live in, roundworms hitch a ride on a beetle to move to a new poop pile.

Dung beetles have special features that make them good at plowing through poo. Their front legs are spiny and flattened, which helps them tunnel into waste. Some species have strong hind legs to push balls of poop around. Dung beetles also use their shovel-like heads to dig through manure and dirt.

The Sweet Smell of Scat

Poop might smell bad to us, but to a dung beetle, that smell means supper is ready. These super smellers use club-shaped antennae on their heads to smell dung piles. Some species can even smell **scat** underground. Other dung beetles can tell what animal made the mess just by the odor.

Once dung beetles smell poop, they fly around until they find it. They need to find manure quickly, before it dries out or is eaten by other animals. Many of these amazing poop detectives are strong fliers. They travel miles to get to their next meal.

scat: animal poop

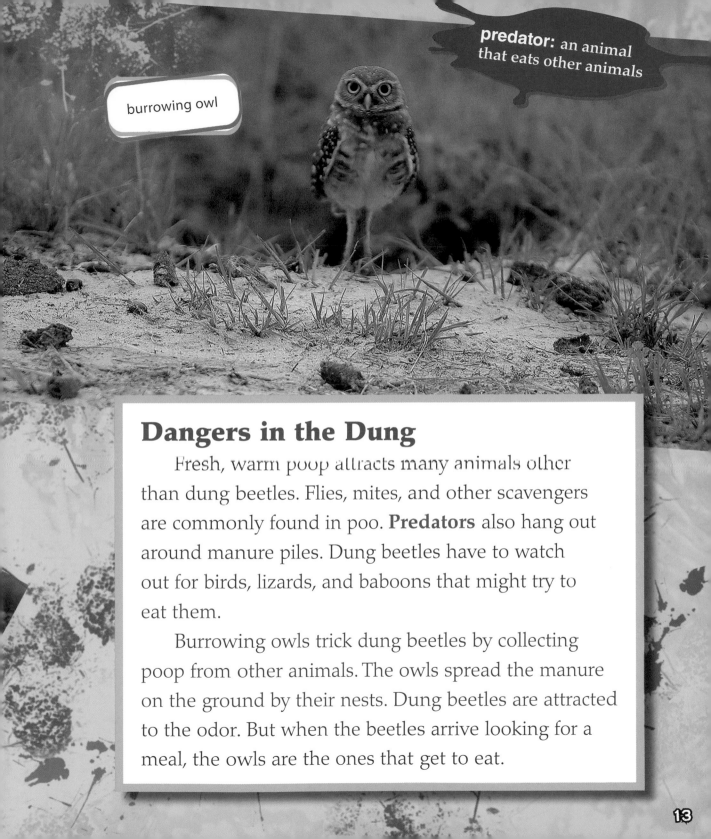

burrowing owl

Dangers in the Dung

Fresh, warm poop attracts many animals other than dung beetles. Flies, mites, and other scavengers are commonly found in poo. **Predators** also hang out around manure piles. Dung beetles have to watch out for birds, lizards, and baboons that might try to eat them.

Burrowing owls trick dung beetles by collecting poop from other animals. The owls spread the manure on the ground by their nests. Dung beetles are attracted to the odor. But when the beetles arrive looking for a meal, the owls are the ones that get to eat.

Development in Dung

You grow up in a home, but dung beetles grow up surrounded by poop. Dung plays an important role in the dung beetle life cycle. Some beetles change from egg to adult without ever leaving a manure pile. Other beetles grow up inside poop balls called brood balls.

dung beetle larva

larva: an insect that has hatched from its egg, but is not yet a pupa

pupa: an insect that has grown out of the larva stage, but is not yet an adult

GROSS!

While they eat their way out of the brood balls, larvae repeatedly eat their own poop.

After adults mate, females lay eggs in poop. **Larvae** hatch from the eggs. Larvae live inside brood balls, and eat the balls from the inside out. Depending on the species, larvae take anywhere from three weeks to five months to change into **pupae**. Pupae don't eat or walk until they turn into adults.

CHAPTER 3

WHAT DO BEETLES DO WITH POO?

Dung beetles spend all their lives in and with poop. But they aren't just playing in it. They use it in many ways to help them survive.

Feces as Food

Poop is the main ingredient in all dung beetle meals. Would you ever think that an insect that eats poop would be picky? Well, to some degree they are. Dung beetles prefer poo from plant-eating animals. Poop from animals that only eat meat is less nutritious.

Not only do they consider where the dung came from, dung beetles also want it to be just the right flavor. Waste comes in a wide range of textures. Many dung beetles prefer to eat soft, runny poop. Others like harder, rougher scat. Some dung beetle adults feed on liquids they squeeze out of manure.

GROSS!

These poop munchers don't stick to just cow or monkey dung. They eat human waste too.

FRESH SQUEEZED POOP JUICE

SERVES: One adult dung beetle

INGREDIENTS: Fresh herbivore dung (can use poop from cows, elephants, monkeys, or other plant-eaters)

STEPS:

1. Crawl onto the warm, smelly mass of droppings.
2. Stretch out mouthparts and scoop up some poop.
3. Press mouthparts together and squeeze the juice out. (Use mouthpart hairs to catch large poop chunks.)
4. Enjoy drinking the liquid poo!

Dwellers

There are four main types of dung beetles. Each type gathers and uses poop a little differently. To dwellers, a big, smelly poop pile is home. These dung beetles like to live in large piles of poo, such as cow pats. Adults and their young live together eating the sticky mess. These dung beetles only leave their poop pile to find a new one.

Tunnelers

Tunnelers don't want other beetles taking their food. They dig nests underneath dung piles. Then they move the poop into these nests. After they've buried the dung, tunnelers shape it into balls and lay their eggs. Some nests have more than 40 balls, and large species can bury more than 5 pounds (2 kilograms) of poop. That's like six cans of soda!

Rollers

Rollers don't like competition. So they take their poop and leave. First, they shape some dung into a ball. Then, using their hind legs, they roll it away. A ball can be 70 times heavier than the beetle!

Rollers are also called tumblebugs. Ancient Egyptians believed that tumblebugs were sacred animals. The Egyptians thought these beetles were special because they moved underground and then came back up again, much like the sun moves.

Thieves

Some dung beetles are called kleptoparasites. Instead of getting their own manure, they steal it from other dung beetles. One type of robber crawls into a nest, destroys the eggs on the buried brood ball, and lays its own eggs.

Some poop thieves steal balls from rollers. They attack rollers and try to run away with the poop ball. Other kleptoparasites fly around until they find a roller moving a poop ball. Then they dive into the tasty ball of poo.

CHAPTER 4

Poop-Eater Power

Dung beetles aren't just the planet's clean-up crew. These super insects help the environment in many other ways.

By eating and burying manure, dung beetles help break waste down and return nutrients to the soil. These beetles mix the soil when they tunnel and bury waste.

People need dung beetles too. In Australia, poop was building up in pastures, so scientists released dung beetles to get rid of the mess and help increase soil fertility. The beetles took care of the dirty job. They also made the soil better for growing plants, improving the area for cattle grazing.

Dung beetles' work keeps the soil healthy and our environment less smelly.

GROSS!

Each year, dung beetles get rid of almost half a ton of poop per acre. That's like eating 1,000 pounds (454 kilograms) of jellybeans in one year.

Interview with a Dung Beetle

Interviewer: Tell me, why do you eat poo? Isn't that a waste product?

Dung beetle: Although it's not good for many other animals, poop is a delicious, healthy meal for me. I eat it all the time and feed it to my kids.

Interviewer: Many people are disgusted by your strong attraction to poop. What would you tell your critics?

Dung beetle: I can't believe people think my behavior is gross! I help clean up after all those messy animals day after day.

Interviewer: Is that the only reason your job is worthwhile?

Dung beetle: Absolutely not! I help plants grow, control harmful pests, and keep the environment clean and safe for humans. People need to realize that my job is really important and show me a little respect.

Sowing Seeds

Many animal droppings contain seeds. As dung beetles roll away poop, they also move seeds. Dung beetles help new plants grow by burying seed-filled poop. Rodents would eat the seeds if dung beetles didn't push them underground.

Pest Control

Dung beetles help people and animals in yet another way. When dung beetles eat manure, they control pests that attack humans and cattle, including bloodsucking flies. Eating dung takes food away from fly larvae and damages fly eggs.

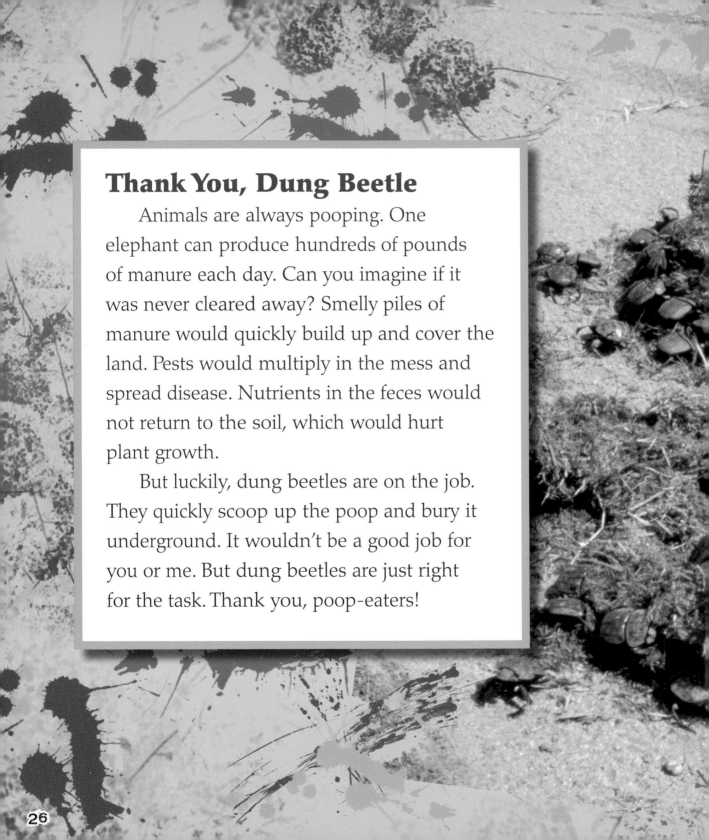

Thank You, Dung Beetle

Animals are always pooping. One elephant can produce hundreds of pounds of manure each day. Can you imagine if it was never cleared away? Smelly piles of manure would quickly build up and cover the land. Pests would multiply in the mess and spread disease. Nutrients in the feces would not return to the soil, which would hurt plant growth.

But luckily, dung beetles are on the job. They quickly scoop up the poop and bury it underground. It wouldn't be a good job for you or me. But dung beetles are just right for the task. Thank you, poop-eaters!

TRUE LIVES OF SCIENTISTS

Wildlife biologists study all kinds of animal behavior. But one of the smelliest research projects is all about the dung beetle. Dung beetles roll seed-filled poop around the rain forest and bury it deep in the ground. That's why some wildlife biologists think dung beetles might be able to help regrow parts of the rain forest that have been cut down.

poop trap

Digging in Dung

How are scientists studying dung beetles burying seeds? They're putting beetles in buckets, watching, and waiting.

The buckets are filled with soil and dung. Scientists place seeds inside the buckets. Then they put in dung beetles. After a couple of days, the scientists slap on gloves and dig through the poo. They look to see what seeds are buried and what beetles buried them. With the information they gather, scientists are hoping to figure out how dung beetles could help replant the rain forest.

Poop Traps

The scientists needed dung beetles for their experiments. How did they get them? They set poop traps! Scientists buried cups in the ground. They hung human poop above the cup. Dung beetles fell into the trap trying to get the poo.

GLOSSARY

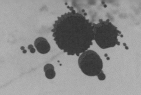

CONSUMER (kuhn-SOO-mur) — an animal that eats plants or other animals for energy

LARVA (LAR-vuh) — an insect at the stage of development between an egg and a pupa when it looks like a worm; more than one larva are larvae.

MANURE (muh-NOO-ur) — animal waste

PREDATOR (PRED-uh-tur) — an animal that hunts other animals for food

PUPA (PYOO-puh) — an insect at the stage of development between a larva and an adult; more than one pupa are pupae.

SCAT (SKAT) — animal droppings

SCAVENGER (SKAV-uhn-jer) — an animal that looks through waste for food

SPECIES (SPEE-sheez) — a specific type of animal or plant

INTERNET SITES

FactHound offers a safe, fun way to find Internet sites related to this book. All of the sites on FactHound have been researched by our staff.

Here's how:

1. Visit *www.facthound.com*

2. Choose your grade level.

3. Type in this book ID **1429612657** for age-appropriate sites. You may also browse subjects by clicking on letters, or by clicking on pictures and words.

4. Click on the **Fetch It** button.

FactHound will fetch the best sites for you!

READ MORE

Hipp, Andrew. *Dung Beetles*. The Really Wild Life of Insects. New York: PowerKids Press, 2003.

Lockwood, Sophie. *Beetles*. The World of Insects. Mankato, Minn.: Child's World, 2007.

Twist, Clint. *Dung Beetles*. Nature's Minibeasts. Milwaukee: Gareth Stevens, 2006.

INDEX